THE SKIN OF YOUR BACK

THE SKIN OF YOUR BACK

Michael Rosen

Five Leaves Publications

The Skin of Your Back

Published in 1996 by Five Leaves Publications,
PO Box 81, Nottingham, NG5 4ER

Published with financial assistance from

Printed by Chas. Goater, Nottingham

ISBN 0 907123 66 X

CONTENTS

Aldermaston March

I ran away from home once.
I was 13
the second year of the Aldermaston March
marching from Aldermaston to London
to Ban the Bomb (for evermore).

I said, I'm going on the Aldermaston March.

They both said that this was out of the question,
the boy's mad, crazy.

My mother said,
where will you stay? you'd have nothing to eat
you don't know anyone, what would you eat?
You're not going.
Harold say something, he's too young,
look at him, he's packing.
You can't go without a spare pair of trousers
how can he carry a bag like that for 20 miles a day?
Stop him Harold
what would you do in the evening?
you need to eat, you get ill if you don't eat
take a tin of beans, you can always eat beans
Harold, stop him.
There's the chicken, take the chicken
if you're taking a tin of beans, take 2
he's thirteen Harold, go next year
wait till next year, they won't have banned the bomb by then,
believe me. There'll be another march, go on that one.
You must keep eating fresh fruit.
And you like dates. he's always liked dates, hasn't he Harold?
Just squeeze them in down the side of the bag.

Couldn't he wait till the last day
when we'll be there?
We can all go to Trafalgar Square together
Harold have you got the chicken?
Just because its Easter doesn't mean it's warm.
It can snow at Easter, wear the string vest.
Who's organised the coaches?
Do we know these people Harold?
One orange! Take five. And raisins.
He's 13. It's ridiculous. He can't go.
Keep the chicken wrapped.
Phone us if you need more food.
Goodbye.

Burglary

I got burgled
they emptied out boxes
ripped open files
took the answer machine
and four harmonicas
not much else
oh yeah
three tapes I made
one was called
Hairy Tales and Nursery Crimes
one was called
Quick Let's Get Out of Here
and one was called
You Can't Catch Me
I suppose burglars have jokes
and I almost laughed...
after all they hadn't stolen much
and they hadn't broken anything...
but then I caught sight of something.
It was the only thing they broke:
they had smashed the glass of
a mounted photo of 18 *hassidim*
in their fur hats and white leggings
standing in Stamford Hill
carrying banners saying:

WE ARE ANTI-ZIONIST BECAUSE WE ARE JEWS

THE JEWS HAVE ALWAYS BEEN KNOWN AS
MERCIFUL

WE REQUEST THAT THE NAME ISRAEL
WHICH BELONGS TO THE JEWISH PEOPLE
MUST BE WITHDRAWN FROM THE ZIONIST STATE

ANTI-ZIONIST IS NOT ANTI-SEMITIC

IF ALL THE ARAB STATES RECOGNISE THE
ZIONIST STATE
WE WOULD STILL OPPOSE IT

It's best not to figure out
exactly what kind of person would want to
steal an answer machine, four harmonicas
three tapes for children with absurdly relevant titles
and also want to
smash a photo like that.

For Jack

Ewan MacColl (father of Kirsty)
folk-singer, song-writer, actor, playwright
and crazed Stalinist
accused the New York Jew in our group
of being a petit bourgeois individualist.

We were shocked.
A petit bourgeois individualist?
It was as bad as that, was it?

MacColl sat in his black leather dentist chair
the anglepoise lighting him from the left.
We sat at his feet.
Peggy Seeger distributed copies of the China Study
Group's
latest explanation of why
millions of Chinese peasants dying
was a Great Leap Forward.

The New York Jewish petit bourgeois individualist
left in tears
but that was OK
because we were building socialism.

Hampstead

It was on Aldermaston that I first met Hampstead life.
First day was the march
from the barbed wire round Aldermaston
to Reading.
As a Harrow East person I was coded
as Magenta
but I was walking with the Muswell Hill
old commies who were Jade.
At eight o'clock at night
I found myself wandering around Reading on my own
in the rain and
my shoulder was aching from the weight of chicken in my
bag.

After an hour or so
I found the Magenta Base, an old infant school,
and bedded down in a classroom
surrounded with alphabet friezes
and labelled clothes pegs.
I opened up one of my tins of beans
when in walked two incredible humans.
They were distinctly female
at least six feet tall.
Their legs were sticks bandaged in denim
hanging out the bottom of black sack jumpers.
Long straggles of hair hung round their faces
and two black smudges marked where their eyes
used to be.
Wasn't this what it meant to be a Beatnik or a Bohemian
or a Student even?
Maybe one day I could meet and know
exciting people like this.

One of them had a huge baying hoarse voice.
Oh look, she said,
there's a boy in here.
And good lord, he's eating baked beans
out of the tin. I say, Boy,
have you got any food for us?
Yes, I've got some chicken.
Did your mummy give you that chicken, Boy?
Yes.

They liked the chicken.
Do you have a sex life, Boy?
Do you masturbate?
Do you think we're sexy, Boy?
They were terrifying.

Then they unrolled a double sleeping bag.
Carol and I are sleeping in this together, Boy.
They climbed into the bag and started
flinging clothes out.
Don't look, Boy.
Have you ever seen a naked woman, Boy?
I couldn't say a thing
and then the bras came flying out.
These are bras, Boy.
I suppose the only time you've seen one of these, Boy
is on your mother's washing line.

What was I going to say
about this in school next week?
How could I make it seem like I came out of this thing
looking good?

They left before me in the morning
and I thought that was the end of it.
But as the march headed on to Slough
and I was back with the Harrow East Magenta crowd
hoping to be noticed by the sister of a friend's sister,
alongside us came the baggage truck.
Leaning out the back was The Sleeping Bag 2.
They waved at chosen people
and did things that made their hair shake a lot.
One of Harrow East's more advanced members
told us, as if revealing a fairly sensational fact,
that the one on the left was Labour MP Anthony Greenwood's daughter.
I spent the night in the same room as her?
The one who was interviewed in *The Observer?*
Just as I was frothing about this
she noticed me.
She leaned out the back of the truck.
Oh there's Boy. Hey Boy. It's us.
Say hallo, Boy. Isn't he a dear?
Thanks again for your mummy's chicken.

It did me no good at all with the sister of the friend's sister.

Hoppy

Most people were sure that Hoppy, the PE teacher
was an ex-Nazi.
Officially, his name was Mr Hawtry
but some of us knew
it was really Albrecht Hauptreif.
He was 60, bald, clipped moustache
with a stage German accent.
If you fidgeted
while he was telling you how to do a squat thrust
he would yell louder than the guards
in *The Colditz Story*
- VOT SINK YOU DO, LEDDIE?

He hated asthmatics
and people with teeth-braces, thick glasses, colds,
dirty kit, spots and excuse notes.
On cross country runs, he would come out
in his Ford Popular, stick a megaphone out the window
and yell:
- PICK UP ZOSE GREAT FLET FEET, LEDDIE.

He told us how when he was a boy
they used to run up mountains for hours
followed by cycling up mountains for more hours
then they covered themselves with grease
dived into icy lakes
and swam like mad for a few more hours.
This story would finish with him yelling:
- AND YOU DON'T VONT TO SHTAND AROUNT
  ON ZE SHTREET CORNER VISS ZE BEGGING
  BOWL,
  DO YOU?

The dangerous left-wing Jewish element in the school
were doubtful if such an obvious ex-Nazi
was entitled to further the aims of the Third Reich
in a North West London grammar school
in the late fifties.

Nor would they believe me when I told them
that my dad had told me
that Albrecht Hauptreif was Swiss
fought with the International Brigade
in the Spanish Civil War
and had a bullet in his right shin.

We got an occasional sighting of the bullet wound
but the nearest we got to confirmation of
the Spanish connection
was during the Cuban Missile Crisis,
when, in the middle of an explanation
of why Russian soldiers march in line better than Americans
he turned to me and said,
- *I sink you know vot my record iss, Rosen.*

Crematorium

Old Jewish Communist funerals
at Golders Green Crematorium
seeing off lifetimes of marches, bazaars and strikes
to the sound of Paul Robeson.
Rows of old shoulders
that had shuddered
when the jaws of Belsen gaped.
Tired feet that had followed the leaders:
war wrong — war right;
man hero, man traitor;
tanks-in good, tanks-in bad.
Feeling cheated by the gulags and Chernobyl.
Sad minds that had blocked tales of
murdered Bolsheviks, disappeared Partisans
and *nomenklatura* privilege.

Hadn't they been right to resist pogroms
and discard the liberation marked for Jews only?
Who had stopped Mosley, supported Mandela,
levered the dockers out of Pentonville?
Was it all *dreck?*

Over eats
Solly would tell the one about Hymie and the Red Cross
Solly, councillor and prisoner for his principles
and Lily, Phil, Sam, Rene, Harry glad to hear him.

Simon and Moishe and Peter and Margot gone
Zhirinovsky 24% of the vote
3 million unemployed
Derek Beackon elected

Robeson sings:
I never died, said he.
I never died, said he.

Learning

m
e
p
b

my
elbow
pushes
beautifully

methane
ethane
propane
butane

and that's the carbon chain.

And here's another one:

u
k
i
r

useless
knowledge
I
remember.

Mask

So I was introduced to her dad,
a Jew of the string quartet variety
whose day job was de-poxing prozzies
in Harley Street.

The next day, she says,
- my father said you're a tribal mask.
- What? African?
- No, Jewish.

For years I tried to find any evidence
that Jews made tribal masks.
I hunted through *Encyclopedia Judaica*
hoping to find a picture.

I figured out what he was on about.
It was just a string quartetty way of saying,
- you don't half look Jewish.

Emile

Emile was our hero
a hard man
- weighed only 4 stone when he came out of Dachau, you know
- they never found out he was a Jew
- why was he in there, then?
- caught blowing up a bridge for the French resistance
- but he's Polish, isn't he?
- had false papers

Emile, wiry, dark, bristle-headed
Buddy Holly glasses, American tee-shirts,
sexy wife, sexy daughter,
hero.

Then a whisper went round.

- you know why he won't talk about Dachau?
- what he did in there
- what did he do?
- what he had to do to survive
- like what?
- Imagine

We Imagined.
Maybe Emile wasn't a hero.
Maybe he was a shit.

I thought that was a bit hard on the guy

until the day after
me and the sexy daughter
bunked off school together
and spent the day in the sun
in the wilder part of Hampstead Heath.

I don't know what he did to the SS in France
and I don't know what he did in Dachau
but he was able to give me a very good idea of
what he'd've liked to have done to me.

Plan

We found two rows of trees behind the new estate.
They curved out from the side of the road
and travelled, a road's-width apart
for some hundred yards,
before ending at someone's garden fence.

Trees didn't grow like that naturally, we said.
They were planted. Definitely planted.

They made a space for us to bowl in
or hide and chase,
and later my brother snogged down there
with the one my parents thought
he was crazy to be going with.
The trees weren't old,
there was no crumbling manor house nearby
or demolished mansion
now covered by the new semis.
Two curving rows of trees
starting by a pavement
ending at a fence.

Then my friend Harrybo solved it.
His dad's friend told his mum
it was the Pinner by-pass.
They never built it.

The cars that dragged into Bridge Street
would have whooshed between the trees
heading for picnics in the Chiltern Hills
or into town to Selfridges, Hamleys
or even London Zoo.

It was a Suburban Plan not finished
an uncompleted Improvement.
One of the dreams that didn't happen
like the row of arches in the middle of a field
in Stanmore; a stranded viaduct
once meant for the Northern Line Link.

And also strangely like those moments after tea
when we sat talking over the dirty plates
and my mother seemed to be saying
that some kind of Plan was lost
when Hitler turned up.

The Job

The BNP announced they would hold
an election meeting in the school
I happened to be working at.
We saw a picture of men
with their brass-tipped union jack poles and leather jackets
marching into the school hall.

On the day four hundred of us gathered outside
the school gate.
The cop-coaches turned up.
Their job was to make the school safe for fascists
so they tried to make a nice avenue
up to the gate.
This took up something like two hours
of grumpy heaving
as they didn't seem to be too keen
on lifting headteachers, vicars and
educational psychologists.
But it didn't work out too good for them
so they evaporated.

Then the news broke that
the cops had come up with a better scheme:
smash the back door of the school in
and usher the fascisti into the building.
The chief cop came out and told us
that it was his job to let a democratic meeting take place
so now we could go in if we wanted to.
Lack of unaninimity broke out at once:
- don't go in, everyone go in, take photos.
The nice avenue formed up for us
and in we went.

Not so fast.

After twenty, they brought down the portcullis.
The size of this public meeting would be limited.
In we went.
Some thirty leather jackets were lined up
alongside the brass tipped union jack poles
and among them,
a small man in a lather was shouting
about great nations.
The flecks of spit were landing
on the wall display
by Akaddus, Sabia and Samantha.

We started clapping and singing.
Lather-man moved up an octave.
So did we.
Then, feeling less than pleased with this reception,
the guys in the leather jackets lowered
the brass-tipped union jack poles
and charged at us.

We stopped clapping and singing
(and breathing)
and turned to the local constabulary for assistance.
As the brass-tips came closer
it was of great interest to note
that at this public meeting
(at which it was surmised
public order was in danger of being disrupted, sir,
and that's why we have taken these precautions)
the number of policemen present was now zero.
So we flew out of that hall
faster than kids run from vomit.
It was even more interesting to note
that the policemen, positioned with great foresight
in the playground
leapt to their duty and started arresting us.

Following this,
they protected the meeting from further disruption
by filling the hall and listening to lather-man,
escorted the gang to the tube station
arrested a few Bangladeshi boys
and retired to the nick
well-pleased
(according to the
Super's letter in *The Guardian*)
with the day's work keeping the peace.

Jamaican at Oxford

When they first started shelling out scholarships
round the old Empire,
David was their worst fear:
a biter of the feeding hand.
He spirited up the magically expanding Action Committee
that grew to engulf the bowler hats and gowns
of the university police.

In the occupation,
he was the first through the wrought iron gates
in his shades and chef's trousers;
caught by *The Times* photographer
as evidence that Malcolm X had hit the dreaming spires.

His girlfriend, Yvonne, was refused service
at Annette's the Hairdressers.
Six weeks of picketing didn't budge Annette:
there were going to be no blacks in her parlour.
So David proposed what he said would be
Britain's first sit-in against the colour bar.
The Ever-expanding Us agreed
that One Hundred would head down to Annette's
next Wednesday.
What with the picketing
Annette had got jittery
and arranged a hot line to the cops,
so we opted for a scattered assembly point.
We added ourselves on to bus queues and sweet-shops.
The area saw a sudden increase in snogging couples.
Yvonne walked into Annette's for a cut.
The signal would be her re-appearance at the door.

The scattered Hundred were holding the door in view
by glancing under their armpits, over newspapers.
The place was heaving
with normality.
Yvonne filled the doorway...

...and from the queues and the benches
the winos' rendezvous and lovers' embraces
we ran for Annette's.
In the rush
the hairdressers became the eye of a whirlpool.
20 got in, the rest sat down outside,
Annette shot out screaming
and came for us with the scissors.
I think the now urbane commentator
on American life, Christopher Hitchens,
got it in the skull;
in a matter of seconds
the wagons turned up, the warning read out
and we were soon being lifted
and thrown in the back.

On the day we appeared in court
we pleaded not guilty to obstruction
on the grounds that it was Annette
who was doing the obstructing.
As we were being fined
another Hundred were facing Annette's scissors
as part of David's rolling sit-in concept.
For weeks, I was up to my eyeballs in David's concepts,
Malcolm X, Fanon, Lumumba and Cabral.
They started turning up in my dreams.

News from Jamaica in the early seventies
was that David had gone to the hills.
It was never necessary to ask what he was doing
in the hills -
it was enough just to mutter significantly
David has gone to the hills.
Then somebody said, David was in jail.
It was getting real.

In 1977, London *Time Out* listings
had David,
General Secretary of the Jamaican Workers Liberation
League
speaking in Paddington.

I went.
He was still wearing shades
but now a suit.
I listened, waiting for the spark,
some new scheme,
an ever-expanding rolling, unstoppable whatsit,
that would release Jamaica and the world from
the machines that had crushed Hanoi and Prague.
No, it wasn't there.
Naive white loony to think it would be.
Get real.

But as I sat puzzling about where the fizz had gone
he used the phrase:
the peace-loving peoples.
In fact he used it again and again.
The pages of *Soviet Weekly* and *GDR News*
(delivered to my parents,
once a fortnight by Bill on his bike)
flickered in front of me.
Smiling peace-loving peoples of Poland,
Romania and the KGB beamed at me.

At the end I said,
- *Hi, how you doing? Remem-*
And he said,
- *I meet a lot of people. Sorry I must go.*

Northumberland

He took me when I was eleven up on the moor
and showed me sheep stuck on their backs.
They roll over to scratch theirselves.
The wool takes up the water
they can't rise.
He grabs a blackface and heaves it out of the hollow.
They die if I don't do that.
You and your mum and dad don't believe in God
do you?

He took me to the stable
and showed me a cow
with a chain round her neck.
Milk fever, he says.
He holds a bottle above her neck,
runs a tube down to a needle.
He jabs the needle into the cow.
A big flat bubble swells up
under the cow's skin
around the root of the needle.
Her eyes roll and whiten.
You're afraid she'll die, aren't you?
I'm not afraid of death.
You are.

He took me into the field
and showed me a cow with her calf
lying in the pool of its afterbirth.
If it doesn't get up
I'll have to take it away.
If I touch it too soon, mind
the cow won't have anything to do with it.
Reject it.

We watched.
Could you kill a man?
I had to choose.
Kill or be killed.
What would you do?
There it's up — it won't need a bottle.
The cow'll eat all that stuff now.
You wouldn't, would you?

Adverbs

Today we have adverbs.
As you can hear an adverb
is something to do with a verb.
You remember the verb from last week?
The adverb tell us how the word we call a verb
does its business.
Except you remember the verb doesn't only *do*
it also *is* and *feels*.
So the adverb tells the verb how.
But also remember a verb isn't strictly speaking
a word.

It can be two, three or even four words.
And also — strictly speaking -
we can't always be certain which of these words
the adverb is telling how to.
OK?
Now the adverb is also a word
that describes adjectives.
You remember adjectives describe nouns.
So really these kind of adverbs should be called
ad-adjectives.
But they're not.
Sorry about that
but there's nothing I can do about that.
Same word — adverb —
doing its stuff to verbs
doing its stuff to adjectives.
But watch out here:
don't go calling any old word
hanging in there next to an adjective
an adverb.
It could be another adjective.
Watch out for that one.

Are you still with me?
Great,
because this gets even more interesting.
Sometimes there are words that
do things to adverbs.
You know what we call them?
Adverbs.
They could
it's true
be called ad-adverbs
but they're not
my hands are tied.

And we might as well
do the job properly here:
there's even another kind of adverb
that is really all on its own but
in a kind of way
does things to the whole of the rest of the sentence.
Don't ask me just for the moment to remind you
what a sentence is
but just remember there is this word
(not actually called an ad-sentence)
that is doing some business for the whole sentence.
And it's an adverb.

So there you are.
Get reading
and look out for adverbs
changing all sorts of things
all over the place.
It's a useful word isn't it?
Adverb.
Once you get the hang of them
they're good fun:

Well, honestly, -
they're really dead easy.

well, adverb
honestly, adverb
really, adverb
dead, adverb

Moishe

One time Moishe,
my friend Chris's dad,
put on a science show
in the laundry-room in the basement of his flats.
It was packed out with friends and relatives.
Moishe was crazy about plastic.
I think I heard him say that one day
everything could be made of plastic.

In the science show,
Moishe poured mercury into liquid oxygen
and the mercury went solid.
He put a soft rubber ball into liquid oxygen
fished it out, threw it on the floor
and it broke into bits.
Then he poured liquid oxygen in the sink
and it boiled.
It was magic. Everybody clapped
and somebody's aunt said,
So this is why you spent all that time at college, Moishe!

I didn't think Chris's mum, Rene,
was quite so passionate about plastic
until one day she served me up fried egg and mushrooms
with a plastic egg.

Why didn't I have a father who could break rubber balls
and a mother who played tricks with plastic eggs?

Bosnia

And after much talking, the bomb stood up and spoke:
Friends, I speak for civilisation and culture
I speak in the great tradition of standing up to fascism
I speak for the rights of small nations
Abyssinia, Czechoslovakia, Poland
I speak in the name of -
(here the bomb lowered his voice)
I speak in the name of the six million Jews

The room fell quiet
a roomful of our generals and leaders
all bearing emblems of peace and goodwill unto all men
all bearing fatigues and armour
blood-spattered from the battlefields
of Belfast, Port Stanley, Panama and Baghdad
all sweating and straining to keep control of their world disorder.

One leapt to his feet.
What can you do for us?
And the bomb replied
I can fly from the sky and find out your enemy
I can seek the culprit
pinpoint the armaments that deal out such pain and misery
and,
like honey on fresh bread,
I can spread peace and comfort to all.

Then our leaders spoke in agreement:
we can select an enemy
we can choose a culprit
we can set your sights
we can show the world
that we can solve problems
we can win respect
we can keep power
we can keep power
we can keep power

Not so fast gentlemen, said the bomb
I am but one.
Before sending me on my mission
you must make many more like me.

No problem
bellowed back our leaders,
each fresh from downsizing a hospital
from taking the slack out of pensions
from slimming down some meals on wheels
no problem
we can make bombs
we can make bombs
go, do your best, make peace.

And the bomb got up and left the room
and did what he has always done
whether it was in Guernica or Dresden
Hanoi or Baghdad
he found out, he sought, he pinpointed
someone driving a bus
someone bathing a wound
someone digging potatoes
someone scrubbing a floor.

And so it is that in the forests and mountains
victims become culprits
culprits become victims
culprits become victims
victims become culprits
and so it is that their generals and leaders
and our generals and leaders
send the starving victim-culprits
down to the shops to stand in queues
to buy guns and shells and tanks -
send them to clean each other off their farms and fields.

And all this time
their generals and leaders
and our generals and leaders
stroll on the lawns of international conference centres
explaining their position vis-à-vis the safe havens
yes, the safe havens,
not intending with that
to refer to their own skins
their own suits
and their own beds.

My Mother at the Undertakers

She was dead
it was before the funeral
when my father said he wanted to go and see her
did I want to come?

She was laid out in the backroom
strangely high
as if on a lab bench
with a sheet up to her chin

my father went in ahead of me
and stood next to her head
I wondered if we were doing this
because we were Jews

her skin shone like an insect
and her nose had shrunk down to a beak
this is all that's left
this is all that's left

I turned away but saw my father
lean in close to her
raise his hands into the space between his face
and hers.
For one moment I thought he was going to clap.
Then it seemed like he was going to hold her head.
Or perhaps his.
But what he did was shake his hands,
shake them in that space between his face
and hers.

It seemed like some ancient gesture
some blessing. Or curse. Or both.
Wishing her a safe passage?
Or cursing her for leaving him.
He stared and muttered
looked away and looked again.
I could see what he was doing:
forcing this picture into his mind,
making himself hold on to this last view of her
after forty years of knowing it like the back of his hand.
Or hers.

Insight

I'm an
in-depth
in-terviewer
for
In-sight
the
in-dependent
in-formation
analysts.
I am
in-credibly
useful.

Heres another piece of research
published in Sunday papers
discussed on *Newsnight*
in which I can prove
that people on housing estates
are

more evil
less literate
more stupid
less married
more addicted
less polite
more violent
less nice
more greedy
less responsible
more perverted
less skilled
more aggressive
less thoughtful
more psychotic
less caring
than me.
Good night.

Republican Hate Poem

May the King
lose his thing.
May the Queen
get gangrene.
May the Prince
be made into mince.
May the Princess
become an abcess.
May all the royals
come up in boils.
The odd Duchess or Duke
can turn into puke.
Same goes for a Knight
who should be reduced to shite.

The Ballad of Roger Ball

Roger was a lefty
lived in a basement flat,
taught slow learners,
wore a soft grey hat.

Roger was a theorist,
found time in between
to hit you with Althusser,
write articles for *Screen*.

Roger loathed marriage,
mortgages and taxis,
said we should solidarise
and always practice praxis.

He convinced some of his colleagues
that capitalism was shitty.
They thought long and deep
then fled the inner city.

There weren't many left
when the idea was floated
that Roger could do better:
Roger was promoted.

The comrades were troubled,
there was a bit of friction.
He said he was a realist
he was facing contradiction.

To make his position clear
he tended to rant and hector.
Then Roger bought a suit.
Roger became an inspector.

He talked software, studied wines,
joined a gym, ran at night,
met Celia, bought the mobile
put it in his Samsonite.

Then one day
when Roger was resting,
he saw the future:
it said: Testing.

Marking, grading,
figures, tables,
checking, assessing
goals, labels.

He'd seen himself as
one of history's liberators.
Now he'd do it with
Performance Indicators.

He solemnly declared
he would never swerve
from giving the masses
what they deserve.

Marking, grading,
figures, tables,
checking, assessing,
goals, labels.

Now equipped
with these ground rules,
he headed down town:
closed two schools.

To which plan he added
important features:
wrote a mission statement
and fired fourteen teachers.

Roger was amazed.
There were strikes and demos.
Roger was furious
he sent off memos:

'This is confidential
but I know the leaders.
They're ex-friends.
Sack the bleeders.'

Roger was tough
Roger was thorough.
Roger brought rigour
to a Labour borough.

Roger brought success
Roger brought glory
and felt insulted
when he was called a Tory.

Well the Rogers of the world
don't always have it easy.
The protests swelled
he came over queasy.

Seems: just as Roger
got slicker and slicker
he put too much pressure
on his all-red ticker.

He packed his bags
he's not exultant
he's now what's called
an Education Consultant.

He travels around.
He helps. He advises
on how to live
with bigger class sizes.

Management teams
are keen to enlist him.
Roger remains as ever
useful to the system.

In French

My words to you
are clipped out of verb-lists
and Excursions to the Beach.
We whisper among white walls
at their darkest time
while upstairs downstairs
ears at the floors and ceilings
adjust their hold.
Words hissing in a space where
I have nothing to tell me that I have offended
your gentle trembling
with Toto dans le jardin.

To explain these shots in the dark
I try some English
and it is you, quiet cat
that becomes that dark behind the shutters
asking me to say again
what I had tried to say
with my lips held against the skin of your back.

Growing

I once had a teacher who said that
the difference between the French and the English
is their gardens,
and every summer term for five years
he drew two straight lines, and said:
French, eg Versailles
and then drew two wiggled ones and said
English, eg Hampton Court.

I also had a teacher who said that
the thing about Mark Antony was that
he had an electric effect over his fellow-man
which was like the Prince of Wales in 1932
when he reviewed the Cambridge OTC
(Officer Training Corps)
and made we chaps want to lie and die for him
which is what Antony did apparently
every year Oxford and Cambridge Exam Board
put him on the A-level syllabus.

We had teachers who recited you make bar magnets
by Stroking
that there wasn't time to be funny in the GCE exam
that if we had had enough sense
we'd've been on the side of the Germans in the last war
that three Lates equalled one Detention
two Detentions equalled one On Report
two On Reports equalled one Suspension
and at some stage after that
the world at large was judged to be the better judge

and that in the first year you lived in the huts
in the third year you stopped wearing caps
in the fifth year you could stay in at dinner time
and in the upper sixth
at the summit of your pinnacle
you might be asked to apply for university
and there, an agnostic priest of a careers master said,
there, over three years of profound daily intercourse
your glorious individualised flower
would finally bloom.

Oxford

Let night come now
and fill these grey panes
let the town blink and stutter
behind the trees
the piano in the room
stop dinking
even two boys like corks
bobbing at their white buoyball
on the lawns
stop
the bells dee dee dow dow
stop please stop
gun down the nibbling nostalgias
that come crawling through
the milk between the trees
bring on some night
disguise the shops
mask heads and hot-dogs vans
keep their details and distance from me
the night will make a shelter
and bed — though single — a shade.

The Woods

Up in the woods
my children begin a conversation about
suicides I have known

the one in the car, exhaust pipe redirected
middle aged man
the one in front of a train at Kings Cross
young man
the one with a gun
middle aged man

one of them was drinking
one found life at university unbearable
one was a lifelong depressive

one hated everybody, especially himself
one had tense shoulders
one thought everyone else in his family
was brilliant

and yet
one was a good a musician
one was a wit
one was a loved dad

up in the woods
I sense the children not asking
how fed up I am these days.

Nativity: now and then

The crib's lit. Shepherds stare.
Out-of-scale straw waits for impossible cattle-turds.
Mary looks like the woman from the Vidal Sassoon ad
Joseph, like me.

I remember this stuff.
I lived next door to St. Lukes
and December hometimes were delayed
when we lingered in the light of it.
Odd that we thought these unmoving plaster dummies
brought the story to life.

We? No.
I knew this wasn't my stuff.
It was theirs.
This Family didn't belong to me.
And even if the wiseguys were foreigners
Mary and Joseph were English, suburban,
from just up the road, had a sitting room
where you weren't allowed to play on Sundays,
spoke like my headteacher.

I envied my friends' treat
their way of warming themselves by the scene
but I didn't know then that she was a Miriam
and he a Yossef.

Trumpington

It was in a bed in Trumpington
that I first heard that cascade of cries
that whoop from low down
that hand at the base of my back
pulling, pushing, skidding, kneading

— *why now?*
— *didn't you feel?*

I had.
She had slowed me down
and way deep inside, pull, hold and breathe
pull, hold and breathe
and it was then it all broke loose about me
a time to roll around my mind -
but for some shame.

Inside six months I was so cocksure
that I went off
wondering if there was joy like this
to be found with someone else.
Damn and curses, damn and curses
that there was no one at my shoulder
to tell me I was trashing pearls.

Loch

you said, why not?
it's cold, so what?
everything off
come on.

and we did

the moors purple
the loch water brown deep earthy
and we were white seals pushing currents
between us
gems of water on our faces
reaching through the cold for fingers for bumcheeks

— look at your nipples
— your balls feel like walnuts

the brown water got through to our bones
and we thrashed our way out
rasped our skin with the towels
and you said, let's have a fuck
and I said, with this?
and we looked at the little mauve mushroom
by the walnuts.
It won't stay like that, you said
and you laid out the towels
and it didn't stay like that

On location

one time having breakfast with Paul
in a small hotel in Dorset, on location
he said, see that couple over there?
well, I have to admire his staying power,
last night they were at it for hours
in the room next door to me
I don't know how he did it
but I admire him, honestly, I admire him.

and we both looked at them
he in his polished brown shoes
and Fred Perry shirt
looking like someone who wanted (but failed)
to get into a cricket team.
Where did he fill his tank, eh?

and her, oh wonders,
I guess,
we both thought long and deep about her
as she sat nibbling cornflakes
what magic lay between her legs?
her hair polite but fluffy
a neat floral dress
a respectable upright pose at the table
no come-ons, no morning smirks,
no fond inseparable hand-squeezing
no surface signs of endless pleasures or
multiple delights in the cricketer's arms.

just the cornflakes, nothing but the cornflakes
and me and Paul wondering and wondering
on the how and why of them
or
if we risked it
wondering on the how and why of
what happens when we
in our bedrooms, in our homes
turn out the light and try and do our best

Bodies

When I was doing anatomy
we had to dissect a human body.
A dead body isn't difficult.
It lies on the table very still:
oozing preservative.
Careful slicing reveals bones and organs
that we know best as metaphors:
he hasn't got the guts,
give it a bit of elbow grease

After one heavy morning investigating ventricles and heart valves,
Dave dumped the whole thing in my hand saying:
Have a heart.

Hardest of all is talking about it.
Is it *my* body?
The tutor calls it *your* body,
as in:

Take the right arm off your body.
or:
How are you getting on with your body.

I would introduce fellow students as
This is Maggie, she works on my body.

After several weeks confusion
we solved it:

We called it Gladys.

Typewriters

The old jazz of typewriters
the bump and slide
go carriage go
the bebop
of QWERTYUIOP
dummm with the thumb
on the space bar
and even the diddle
(the little fiddle)
with the ribbon
that didn't-didn't.
So whirl the wheel
ink your fingers
glimpse the fluff
all that fluff
down in the deep with
the teeth, the rows of teeth
that smacked and clacked
then, oh bugger — stuck

but

never wiped
never lost the lot
never turned word into void
never vanished text into the next

just delivered up
its mistakeful old stuff
its grils and boys
could even dish it up twice
and thrice
when I was flush enough
to buy
oh say it
self-carbonating paper
one more time
self-carbonating paper.
Take a copy, guys.

ALSO AVAILABLE FROM FIVE LEAVES PUBLICATIONS

YOU ARE, AREN'T YOU?

by Michael Rosen

72 pages, £4.99, paperback, 0 907123 09 0

A collection of Jewish and socialist poems. As *haimish* as a pickled cucumber, and as sharp.

THE DYBBUK OF DELIGHT: AN ANTHOLOGY OF JEWISH WOMEN'S POETRY

Edited by Sonja Lyndon and Sylvia Paskin

236 pages, £9.99, flapped paperback, 0 907123 57 0

A major celebration of Jewish women's creativity, covering the interests of contemporary Jewish women, religious and secular. 62 contributors including Elaine Feinstein, Ruth Fainlight, Rabbi Elizabeth Sarah, Michelene Wandor, Wanda Barford, Lotte Kramer, Valerie Sinason and Sue Hubbard.

The Dybbuk of Delight is a remarkable collection of poems: passionate, witty, often heartbreaking.
Ham and High

LAUGHING ALL THE WAY

by Liz Cashdan

72 pages, £5.99, paperback, 0 907123 46 5

Liz Cashdan's poems convey a strong sense of personal identity and include the acclaimed Tyre-Cairo letters, a dramatic reconstruction of the life of an 11th century Jewish family.

THE SHALLOW GRAVE: A MEMOIR OF THE SPANISH CIVIL WAR

by Walter Gregory

192 pages, £6.99, paperback, 0 907123 61 9

To read Walter Gregory's memoir is to breathe again the heady air of myth and belief... and to know that for the generation of the 1930s, their Spanish Civil War will never end.
Daily Telegraph

WATER
by Sue Thomas
162 pages, £7.99, paperback, 0 907123 51 1
"In the end she was forced to take her chances on the open ocean and there, off the coast of Scotland, she drowned him because she thought he deserved it. He probably did..."
Fiction

DESTROYING THE BABY IN THEMSELVES: WHY DID THE TWO BOYS KILL JAMES BULGER?
by David Jackson
46 pages, £3.50, paperback, 0 907123 31 7
That blurred, foggy frame of the security video has become engraved on the public conscience. We can never know the whole truth of what followed, but a critical re-focussing on the Bulger case is essential if we are to challenge the paralysing horror of the event.

THIS IS NO BOOK: A GAY READER
by Gregory Woods
112 pages, £6.95, paperback, 0 907123 26 0
A collection of review essays by one of Britain's leading authorities on gay men's literature.

FORTHCOMING TITLES FROM FIVE LEAVES PUBLICATIONS INCLUDE:

POEMS FOR THE BEEKEEPER

Edited by Robert Gent

96 pages, £5.99, available October 96, paperback 0 907123 82 1

An introduction to the range of modern poetry in Britain today, celebrating fifteen years of poetry performances in Beeston, Nottingham.

Contributors include Dannie Abse, James Berry, Alan Brownjohn, Wendy Cope, Robert Creeley, Kwame Dawes, U. A. Fanthorpe, John Lucas, Roger McGough, Adrian Mitchell, Henry Normal, Brian Patten, Tom Paulin, Peter Redgrove, Jon Silkin and many more.

THE JEW, THE ELEPHANT AND THE CITY

Edited by Sonja Lyndon and Sylvia Paskin

Contemporary short stories on urban life by modern Jewish writers (forthcoming, November 96).

READING THE BEANO AND OTHER STORIES

by Michael Rosen

Collected essays on children's literature (forthcoming, October 96).

DID I HEAR YOU WRITE?

by Michael Rosen

A new edition of his standard text on using poetry in schools (forthcoming, October 96).

THE RADICAL 20s

by John Lucas

Examining popular culture and literature of the 1920s (forthcoming, Feb 97).

All books published by Five Leaves are available through bookshops or, post free, from PO Box 81, Nottingham, NG5 4ER. Trade orders UK and Europe/Central Books, USA and Canada/AK Press.